Cultural Crafts

THE CULTURE AND CRAFTS OF
ITALY

Paul Challen

PowerKiDS press™

Published in 2016 by **The Rosen Publishing Group, Inc.**
29 East 21st Street, New York, NY 10010

Developed and produced for Rosen by BlueAppleWorks Inc.

Art Director: T. J. Choleva
Managing Editor for BlueAppleWorks: Melissa McClellan
Designer: Joshua Avramson
Photo Research: Jane Reid
Editor: Rachel Stuckey
Craft Artisans: Eva Challen (p. 7, 21), Jane Yates (p. 17), Jerrie McClellan (p. 25)

Photo Credits:
Cover top left ermess/Shutterstock; cover top middle left Viacheslav Lopatin/Shutterstock; cover top middle right astudio/
Shutterstock; cover top right Marco Cannizzaro/Shutterstock; cover middle Joshua Avramson/Shutterstock images;cover
bottom images, p. 6–7, 16–17, 20–21, 24–25, 27 bottom right Austen Photography; cover top, title page top Daboost/
Shutterstock; back cover, p. 4 top Arid Ocean/Shutterstock; title page Gandolfo Cannatella/Dreamstime; p. 4 bottom Michal
Ninger/Shutterstock; p. 5 bottom bonilla/Shutterstock;p. 5 middle Samot/Shutterstock; p. 5 right saras66 /Shutterstock;
p. 8 top, 8–9 Utente:Jollyroger/Creative Commons; p. 9 right Andrey Omelyanchuk/Dreamstime; p. 10 top Orietta Gaspari/
Shutterstock; p. 10 bottom Stefano Tinti/Shutterstock; p. 11 left Danilo Mongiello/Dreamstime; p. 11 right vesilvio /
Shutterstock;p. 12 left Gandolfo Cannatella /Dreamstime;p. 12 top Francesco Carucci/Shutterstock; p. 13 left, 23 right Jorg
Hackemann/Shutterstock; p. 13 right United States Library of Congress's Prints and Photographs/Public Domain; p. 14 top
Melodia plus photos/Shutterstock; p. 14 bottom Bryan Busovicki/Shutterstock; p. 15 left Venturelli Luca/Shutterstock; p. 15
right Melodia plus photos /Shutterstock; p. 18 top Andrei Rybachuk/Shutterstock; p. 18 bottom Fabio Bernardi/Dreamstime;
p. 19 left leoks/Shutterstock; p. 19 right Fedor Selivanov /Shutterstock; p. 22 top Ermess /Dreamstime; p. 22 bottom, 23
left Gandolfo Cannatella/Shutterstock; p. 23 top Marco Cannizzaro /Shutterstock; p. 26 top Stefano Tinti /Shutterstock;
p. 26–27 Seregam/Shutterstock; p. 27 top T photography/Shutterstock; p. 28 top Paolo Bona/Shutterstock; p. 28 bottom
Antonio Ros/Dreamstime; p. 29 top cjmac/Shutterstock; XXp. 29 bottom L'irlandés/Creative Commons.

Cataloging-in-Publication-Data

Challen, Paul.
The culture and crafts of Italy / by Paul Challen.
p. cm. — (Cultural crafts)
Includes index.
ISBN 978-1-4994-1123-2 (pbk.)
ISBN 978-1-4994-1133-1 (6 pack)
ISBN 978-1-4994-1161-4 (library binding)
1. Italy — Juvenile literature. 2. Italy — Social life and customs — Juvenile literature.
3. Handicraft — Italy — Juvenile literature. I. Challen, Paul C. (Paul Clarence), 1967-. II. Title.
DG417.C44 2016
945—d23

Manufactured in the United States of America
CPSIA Compliance Information: Batch #WS15PK: For Further Information contact: Rosen Publishing, New York, New York at 1-800-237-9932

Contents

The Country of Italy

Italy is a country on the southern part of the continent of Europe. Most of Italy is surrounded by the Mediterranean and Adriatic Seas. It shares borders with France, Switzerland, Austria, and Slovenia. About 56 million people live in Italy. Italy is a democracy, meaning that the people vote for the government they want to lead them.

Although the "official" form of Italian is spoken by just about everyone in the country, there are many variations, called dialects, spoken in different regions of the country. Dialects use different words, expressions, and pronunciations of the same language – sometimes speakers of one Italian dialect can't understand speakers of another Italian dialect!

The wolf is the national animal of Italy. There are about 500 wolves living in the wild.

Long History

The Ancient Roman civilization was in what we now call Italy. Until about the middle of the 17th century, Italy was one of the main centers of culture in the Western world. During the **Renaissance**, from the 14th to the 17th centuries, Italy led the way in painting, poetry, sculpture, science, and architecture. Famous Italian explorers were some of the first Europeans to visit the New World.

Today, the world is familiar with Italian art, fashion, music, and cuisine, especially the popular **pizza** and **pasta**. Italy is a very popular place for tourists to visit throughout the year.

Florence was home to many Renaissance philosophers, artists, and architects. Today the city celebrates its history.

The Colosseum is a famous ruin of Ancient Rome.

Craft to Make ● ● ● ● ● ● ● ● ● ●

Italians have always used clay or ceramic pots to store things like water and olive oil. Other pots were used to grow flowers and herbs for cooking. It is common for these pots to have colorful designs painted on them.

1 Find a clay terra-cotta pot that you can paint. They come in many sizes, choose one that you will be comfortable painting.

2 Cover your work area with paper. To create a background, paint your pot with white or another light-colored paint.

3 Paint some colorful stripes around the edges of the pot. Paint a pattern along the top. Try using a sponge brush to make lines.

4 Draw your flowers very lightly with pencil. Paint the flowers and leaves with different colors of paint.

5 Outline the flowers with black marker. To complete the Italian theme, use your pot to plant some basil!

You'll Need

- Clay pots
- Paint (assortment of colors)
- Paintbrushes
- Black marker

National Holidays

Republic Day (*festa della Repubblica*) is a national holiday in Italy celebrated on June 2 every year. Italians celebrate this day to remember an important date in their history. In 1946, following the end of the World War II, the Italian people voted on the kind of government they wanted. Some people voted for a monarchy, or rule by a king or queen. But the majority of Italians chose a republic, or democratic government. There is a big military parade in Rome every year to mark *la festa della Repubblica*. Many smaller cities and towns also have parades and celebrations.

The president of Italy presides over the Republic Day parade in Rome.

The Liberation Day

Another popular national holiday in Italy is the Liberation Day, or festa della Liberazione, which is held every April 25. It marks the end of the **Nazi occupation** of Italy in 1945, towards the end of the World War II. Liberation Day remembers the Italian Resistance who fought against the Nazis and Mussolini during World War II. In most Italian cities there are marches and parades to commemorate the event.

DID YOU KNOW

Although Italy is an ancient land, it did not become a country until the late 1800s. Before that, Italy was made up of independent city-states. During a time known as *il Risorgimento* (the "Resurgence"), leaders such as Giuseppe Mazzini and Giuseppe Garibaldi worked to bring these states together. In 1871, Rome became the capital of Italy. Most people consider 1871 to be the birth date of modern Italy.

Giuseppe Garibaldi is famous for uniting the **city-states** of Italy into a single country. Many cities have statues honoring Garibaldi.

Religious Festivals

Italians celebrate the Christmas season with lights and decorations.

The majority of Italians are Christians and followers of the Roman Catholic faith. The **Pope** is the head of the Catholic Church and lives in the **Vatican**, an independent city-state inside the city of Rome.

The two most important religious celebrations in Italy are Christmas (*il Natale*) and Easter (*la Pasqua*).

Panettone is a popular cake that Italians enjoy during the Christmas and New Year's season.

Festive Season

Italians celebrate Christmas in the same way as Christians around the world. Large meals and gift-giving are important parts of an Italian family Christmas. Nativity scenes showing the birth of Christ are also popular.

Twelve days after Christmas is Epiphany (*l'Epifania*). In Italian tradition, an old woman named la Befana visits homes the night before the Epiphany to put treats and gifts in the shoes of young children. She is the Italian Santa Claus!

In the spring, Italians observe Lent and the religious gatherings of Holy Week. Then, on Easter Sunday, they celebrate with feasts and family and religious gatherings on the Sunday that has been chosen for that holiday. Many Italians also celebrate *la Pasquetta* or "little Easter" on the Monday after.

Parades celebrating la Befana are held across Italy on the morning of Epiphany day. People dress in witch costumes and carry big Befana dolls with them.

11

Celebrating Italian Music

Italians have been music lovers since the early Roman times. There are many kind of Italian folk songs. Italians sing songs for special occasions like Christmas and weddings. There are also special folk songs for fisherman, shepherds, and soldiers. Popular and classical music are both well-loved today. Many famous composers such as Giuseppe Verdi, Gioacchino Rossini, and Giacomo Puccini are Italian.

Italians are well known for their love of music and dance.

Italian Opera

The most famous Italian musical form is opera. Opera originated in Italy in the late 16th century. Opera uses a combination of singing, acting, and orchestral music to tell a story. Many operas tell romantic stories. There are many world-famous Italian opera singers like Enrico Caruso, Maria Calas, and Luciano Pavarotti.

Italy is home to many famous opera festivals. One of the best-known is the *Il Maggio Musicale Fiorentino*, which takes place every spring and summer in Florence. This is one of the oldest annual music celebrations in the world.

Canzone Napoletana

The city of Naples is an important part of Italy's musical history. The *canzone napoletana*, or Neapolitan song, is a traditional form of music sung in the Neapolitan dialect. One of the most famous Neapolitan songs is "O Sole mio." During the late 1800s and early 1900s, emigrants from Naples and southern Italy brought the songs to the rest of the world. The *canzone napoletana* also became popular thanks to famous opera singers like Enrico Caruso. After his performances at the Metropolitan Opera in New York, Caruso would sing Neapolitan songs as an **encore**.

Giuseppe Verdi is was one of the best opera composers of the 19th century. His opera *Aida* is still very popular today.

Caruso was one of the most famous performers of his day and helped make Italian music world-famous.

The Venice Carnival

The Venice Carnival is one of the oldest festivals celebrated in Italy. The Carnival takes place in the city of Venice during winter, and lasts for two weeks.

Venice Carnival began in the 15th century. The event allowed all Venetians, rich or poor, to celebrate together. The streets of Venice Carnival were full of people in masks, so you could not tell the difference between the **nobility** and the common people.

Soon the nobility from all over Europe started to attend the Venice Carnival.

The first costumes worn were cloaks with long-nosed masks.

Tradition Continues

Today, the Carnival attracts tourists from all over the world. Venice is one of the most magical cities in Europe. During the Carnival, the city is full of of masked party-goers—posing, dancing, and having fun. Hotels, theaters, cafés, and restaurants welcome thousands of **revelers** with food and entertainment. Carnival is a re-invention of a great historic Venetian tradition.

St. Mark's Square is the main square in Venice. It is also the center of the Carnival activities. You will find the most extraordinary costumes in St. Mark's. Some people hope to win in the best costume competition, some want to be photographed, and others are just there to enjoy themselves.

DID YOU KNOW

The name Carnival, or *Carnevale*, took its name from the Latin words for "meat" (*carnem*) and "farewell" (*vale*). It was a reference to the Church's ban on eating meat during Lent, which is a Christian religious observance. *Carnevale* was the last celebration and feast before Lent began.

The best Carnival costumes and masks can be seen at St. Mark's Square.

Craft to Make • • • • • • • • • • •

Make your own Venice Carnival mask. You can wear it on Halloween, or wear it just to amaze your friends and family at birthday parties and fun get-togethers.

1 Fold a piece of cardstock in half. From the folded edge, draw half of your mask, including an eye hole. While keeping the cardstock folded, cut the mask out. Unfold it and cut both eyes out.

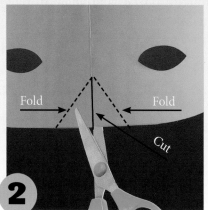

2 Cut along the fold line to just below the eyes. Fold the cut paper forward.

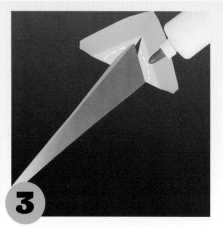

3 Make a nose by drawing and cutting out a triangle on another piece of cardstock. Fold the top half of the triangle in half. Glue it to the folds on the mask.

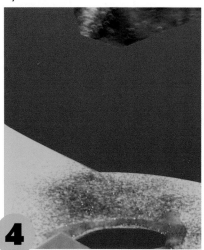

4 Decorate the mask with glitter. Apply glue to the mask. Sprinkle glitter over the glue. Repeat with a different color of glitter. Tap the mask over a sheet of paper to remove the extra glitter.

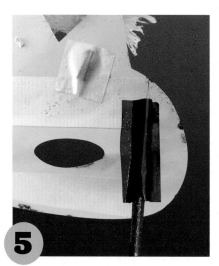

5 Add feathers. Poke holes along the top of the mask. Push one or two feathers through each hole. Tape the feathers to the back of the mask. Paint a dowel. Tape the dowel to the back of your mask.

You'll Need

Cardstock
Pencil
Scissors
Glue
Glitter
Feathers
Wooden dowel or pencil
Tape

Use the dowel to hold the mask in front of your face and have some fun with it!

Traditional Architecture

Italian cities are well-known for their beautiful buildings. The country's architects are famous all over the world for their amazing designs.

Because of Italy's religious tradition, many of its greatest buildings are churches and cathedrals. Examples of this are the Duomo di Milano or Cathedral of Milan, and the many spectacular buildings that make up the Vatican in Rome, such as St. Peter's Basilica.

Duomo di Milano is the fifth largest cathedral in the world and the largest in Italy.

Medieval Hilltop Towns

The hilltop town is another well-known form of Italian architecture. During the **Middle Ages**, people built their settlements on top of the hills of central Italy. For extra protection, townspeople also built defensive walls around their towns. The walls have large gates and watchtowers. Many people still live in these medieval towns. Some of the most well-known hill towns are San Gimignano and Siena in Tuscany and Assisi in Umbria.

Slanting Toward Fame

The Leaning Tower of Pisa is one of Italy's most famous buildings. Pisa is a town in northern Italy. The tower took two centuries to build and was completed in 1372.

Because of a weak foundation and soft ground, the tower started to lean to the side during construction. Today the tower leans very far and keeps moving about half an inch a year. Authorities in Pisa work to make sure the tower will not fall down. But the town will never try to fix the tower. About 1 million people visit the town each year to see the Leaning Tower!

The Leaning Tower of Pisa was built in three stages over 199 years.

Italian hill towns have looked the same for hundreds of years. It's almost impossible to expand or rebuild on top of the hills.

19

Craft to Make ● ● ● ● ● ● ● ● ● ● ● ● ●

Since early Roman times, Italians have used an art form known as the mosaic. To make a mosaic, the artist places many small colored tiles on a sticky surface to make a picture. Mosaics often cover entire walls or floors and can show brightly-colored scenes. It takes a lot of skill and a careful eye to create a mosaic!

1 Gather some dry flat lasagna noodles. Paint each one a different color and let it dry. (You can use cardboard instead of pasta.)

2 Break the painted pasta into various small shapes and sizes. (If using cardboard, cut the cardboard with scissors.)

3 Trace the shape of the frame on a sheet of paper. Lay out the mosiac pieces and move them around until you are happy with the design.

4 Paint the frame if you want to change the color. Apply glue to the frame. Move a piece from the paper to the same position on the frame. Repeat until all the pieces are glued to the frame.

5 Put some glue into a small container. Add a few drops of water to the glue and mix together. Brush the glue over the frame to protect the mosaic pieces. Make sure the glue water is spread around evenly.

You'll Need

Wood frame

Lasagana noodles (or cardboard)

Paint, different colors

Paintbrush

Glue

Paper

Water

Container

Traditional Clothing

Because Italy has many different regions, there are many different types of traditional dress. In the chilly north, costumes can include alpine hats and jackets. In the warmer south, colorful dresses, suits, and hats are common.

Many of these costumes come from the clothing people in the different regions wore for the work that they did, such as farming or fishing.

Italy is the center of the modern fashion world. But many people wear traditional clothes on festive occasions.

Colorful Sicily

It's not just tradititional clothing that changes from region to region in Italy. Pottery, farming equipment, and fishing boats are decorated differently, depending on a region. The island of **Sicily** is well known for colorful pottery and painted carts covered in many colors. Even the horses, mules, and donkeys that pull the carts are draped in bright gear. Many of the fishing villages in Sicily also have brightly colored boats in their harbors.

Gondolas of Venice

The city of Venice, in the north of Italy, is a city of canals. The city was originally built on the land around the Venice Lagoon. To protect against flooding, the houses were built on piles or stilts under the water. Now the city is made of hundreds of man-made islands.

These islands are connected by canals and bridges. The only practical way to get around is by boat. The most famous Venetian boats are called gondolas. These are driven by men called **gondoliers.** Gondoliers are famous for their broad-brimmed hats, striped shirts, and the oars they use to move the boats forward.

The craft of making and decorating carts is handed down from generation to generation.

Craft to Make · · · · · · · · · · · · · ·

Many of the gondoliers who operate the famous boats of Venice wear traditional costumes. Their hats have large white brims and red ribbons.

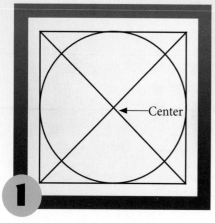
Center

1
Draw a square shape on a piece of cardboard with sides measuring 13 inches (30.5 cm). Draw diagonal lines from corner to corner to pinpoint the center of the square. Draw and cut out a 13-inch (30.5 cm) circle from the cardboard.

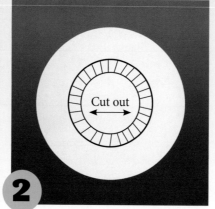
Cut out

2
Draw a 6-inch (15 cm) circle from the center. Draw a 5-inch (13 cm) circle. Mark lines connecting the circles as shown above. Cut the smaller circle out. Cut along the lines just reaching the edges of the larger circle to form tabs. Lift the tabs up.

Cut tabs to line

3
Draw and cut out a 21-inch X 3½-inch (53.3 cm X 9 cm) rectangle from white cardstock to make the side band of the hat. Mark a line 1 inch (2.5 cm) from the edge. Cut tabs to this line.

You'll Need

White poster board or cardboard

White cardstock (or bristol board)

Tape

Red ribbon, 1.5 inches (4 cm) wide

Double-sided tape

Glue dots

*If using ordinary cardboard paint it white before adding the ribbon

4
Draw and cut out a 6¼-inch (16 cm) circle from the poster board to make the top part of the hat. Glue the edges of the side band parts together to form a tube shape. Get all three parts ready to stack as shown above.

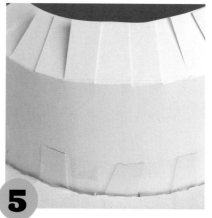

5
Fit the side band to the brim. Alternate the tabs, one inside the brim, one outside. Tape the tabs in place both inside and out.

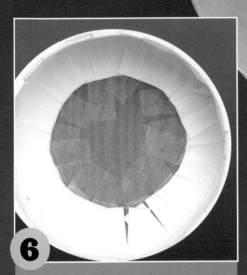

6

Fit the top part to the side band. Put double-sided tape along the edge of the underside of the circle. Place it over the brim and tape the bent tabs to the circle.

Glue

7

Cut one 21-inch (53.3 cm) piece of ribbon. Cut one 33-inch (84 cm) piece. Fold the long piece in half. Wrap the short piece around the crown of the hat just above the brim, glue it together. Loop the long piece behind the short one. Put some glue on the brim piece and fold the long piece over.

Famous Italian Cuisine

The dish we call pizza was invented in Naples, Italy.

Pasta is a staple of Italian cuisine. Italians have been eating pasta for over 800 years!

You cannot talk about life in Italy without talking about food. Italians have introduced the world to two classic dishes — pasta and pizza, which can now be found just about everywhere. Olive oil and wine have been part of the Italian diet since Roman times. And one of the most popular ways to serve coffee, the espresso, originated in Italy as well.

Regional Delicacies

Pizza and pasta may be famous, but Italian food varies from region to region. Each part of the country has its own special foods, based on what grows there.

For example, northern Italian food uses more rice and potatoes. But southern Italian food uses more corn and wheat. Meat dishes throughout the country include chicken, pork, beef, and rabbit. And because Italy is surrounded by the Mediterranean Sea on one side and the Adriatic on the other, fish and seafood such as cod, squid, and shrimp are popular.

Italian cured meats and hard cheeses are famous around the world.

Pasta Necklace Craft

What you need:
- Dried pasta with holes
- Food coloring
- Zip plastic bags
- Paper towels
- String or cord

Place dried pasta in a zip plastic bag.

Pour in 3-4 drops of food coloring. Close the bag and shake it. Shake it until all the pasta is coated. Place the colored pasta on a paper towel to dry. Food coloring can stain, so be careful. Wait for it to dry and then string it on a cord to make a necklace. Tie the ends and make a knot.

Favorite Sports in Italy

Italians love sports, and the one they love the best is soccer, or *il calcio*. Twenty teams from all over the country compete in Italy's top soccer league, with thousands of teams taking part in lower leagues. The Italian national team, known as **Gli Azzurri** (or "the blues"), is one of the most successful national teams in the history of the World Cup. Gli Azzurri has won the World Cup four times, most recently in 2006.

Many boys and girls in Italy play soccer and are fans of pro teams.

Sporty Nation

Italians are also passionate about cycling, auto racing, and basketball.

The Giro d'Italia (Tour of Italy) is a very popular bicycle race that takes place in Italy every summer. The cities compete for the **privilege** to be the starting point for the race. The first Giro was run in 1908. As the Giro gained in popularity the race was lengthened to 21-day-long races. Cyclists from all over the world compete in the race.

Italian teams and drivers have always been successful in Formula 1 auto racing. Italy also has a professional basketball league that is highly regarded internationaly.

DID YOU KNOW

Car enthusiasts know that Italy is famous for the **Ferrari** brand of car. As well as being a fast and stylish ride on the streets, Ferraris are also successful in competition. Team Ferrari (la Scuderia Ferrari) is the most successful Formula 1 team of all time!

Bicycle road racing is one of the most popular sports in Italy.

GLOSSARY

city-state An independent city within a country.

encore A call by an audience at the end of a concert to request an additional performance.

Ferrari The classic Italian sports car. Ferrari is also very successful as a Formula 1 racing team.

Gli Azzurri The nickname of the Italian national soccer team. The teams uniform are azure blue.

gondolier A person who drives a Venetian gondola.

Middle Ages A period of European history from the 5th to the 15th century.

Nazi Occupation A period of time during World War II when a country was being occupied by Nazi forces.

nobility People belonging to the highest social class in a country.

pasta A well-known Italian food made from water, flour and sometimes eggs. Pasta can take many forms, including spaghetti and linguine.

pizza One of the most famous Italian dishes, popular around the world.

Pope The bishop of Rome and leader of the Catholic Church around the world.

privilege A special opportunity to do something that makes you proud.

Renaissance The historical period from about the 14th to the 17th centuries. The Renaissance in Italy was an important time for the growth of arts and culture in Europe.

reveler A person who is enjoying themselves in a lively and noisy way.

Sicily A large island located off the southeast corner of Italy.

Vatican The official residence of the pope in the Vatican City.

Further Reading

Anderson, Robert. *National Geographic Countries of the World: Italy.* Des Moines, IA: National Geographic Children's Books, 2009.

Lonely Planet. *Not For Parents Rome: Everything You Ever Wanted to Know (Lonely Planet Not for Parents).* Oakland, CA: Lonely Planet, 2011.

Matthew, John. *Foods of Italy (Culture in the Kitchen).* Buffalo, NY: Gareth Stevens Publishing, 2011.

Throp, Claire. *Italy (Countries Around the World).* Portsmouth, NH: Heinemann, 2011.

Websites

Due to the changing nature of Internet links, PowerKids Press has developed an online list of websites related to the subject of this book. This site is updated regularly. Please use this link to access the list: **www.powerkidslinks.com/cc/italy**

INDEX